Young Clara Barton

Battlefield Nurse

A Troll First-Start® Biography

by Sarah Alcott

illustrated by Benrei Huang

Troll Associates

Library of Congress Cataloging-in-Publication Data

Alcott, Sarah.
    Young Clara Barton: battlefield nurse / by Sarah Alcott;
illustrated by Benrei Huang.
        p.   cm.— (A Troll first-start biography)
    Summary: Follows the life of the nurse who served on the
battlefields of the Civil War and later founded the American Red
Cross.
        ISBN 0-8167-3766-5 (lib. bdg.)   ISBN 0-8167-3767-3 (pbk.)
        1. Barton, Clara, 1821-1912—Juvenile literature.   2. Red Cross—
United States—Biography—Juvenile literature.   3. Nurses—United
States—Biography—Juvenile literature.   4. United States—History
Civil War, 1861-1865—Medical care—Juvenile literature.
[1. Barton, Clara, 1821-1912.   2. Nurses.   3. Women—Biography.]
I. Huang, Benrei, ill.   II. Title.   III. Series.
HV569.B3A6   1996
361.7'634'092—dc20
[B]   95-8110

Clara Barton was a brave woman. She
carried supplies and medicine to injured
soldiers during the Civil War. She also
started the American Red Cross, a group
that helps people in need.

3

Clarissa Harlowe Barton was born in Massachusetts on December 25, 1821. Everyone called her Clara.

She was the baby of the family. Clara had
two sisters and two brothers.

Clara loved to hear her father tell stories.
He had lots of adventures as a soldier on
the frontier.

Soon it was time for Clara to start school. There was only one school in town, with only one room. She was a good student.

Clara's favorite subject was geography.
She loved to look at maps.

Clara was shy. It was hard for her to make friends.

But she wasn't shy when people needed help. When she was 11 years old, her brother fell off the barn roof and was badly hurt. Clara was his nurse for the two years it took him to get well.

When she was 17 years old, Clara decided to help other children learn. So she became a teacher.

Some of Clara's students were almost her
age. But she was a good teacher and all of
her students loved her.

She was a teacher for 18 years. Then, in 1854, Clara moved to Washington, D.C. She became the first female clerk in the United States Patent Office.

At that time, slavery existed in the
Southern states but not in most Northern
states. Should slavery be allowed? No one
could agree.

The country was so divided over slavery that in 1861 the Civil War began between the North and the South. Young men everywhere volunteered to fight.

15

There were terrible battles. Many soldiers were hurt or killed. Clara wanted to help.

She remembered taking care of her
brother years ago. She knew she would be
good at caring for the wounded soldiers.

Clara was good at reading maps. She memorized military maps so she could find soldiers who needed help.

She wasn't afraid to go on the battlefield. And she didn't care if the soldiers were fighting for the North or the South. She just wanted to help them get well.

Clara brought the soldiers medicine and dressed their wounds. Her bravery and caring saved many lives.

Taking care of soldiers cost a lot of money.
Clara needed other people to help her.

Clara was still shy, but the need for raising
money made her bold. She asked people
everywhere to help. Money was needed to
buy bandages, medicine, food, clothing,
soap, towels, and other supplies for the
wounded soldiers.

People all over the country heard about Clara. They called her the "Angel of the Battlefield" because of her good work.

23

Finally, in 1865, the Civil War was over!
But Clara still had work to do.

President Lincoln asked Clara if she could
form a group that would search for
missing soldiers. She was happy to help.

Four years passed and Clara needed a
rest. She decided to visit Switzerland.

While Clara was in Europe, the Franco-Prussian War broke out. She helped the European soldiers just as she had helped the American soldiers.

In Switzerland Clara met the International
Committee of the Red Cross. This group
helped people in need. Clara thought
America needed the Red Cross, too.

So, in 1881, after she came back to the
United States, she started the American
Red Cross. Many people joined. Clara
taught them everything she knew about
helping others.

Today, the American Red Cross is always ready to help when there are hurricanes, floods, and other disasters.

Clara Barton died in 1912. She will always
be remembered as a brave and heroic
woman, in war and in peace.